Exuberant Light
60 Day Faith Igniter Devotional

Kendra Thorpe

Written By: Kendra Thorpe

© 2020

ALL RIGHTS RESERVED. No part of this book may be reproduced in any written, electronic, recording, or photocopying without written permission of the publisher or author. The exception would be in the case of brief quotations embodied in the critical articles or reviews and pages where permission is specifically granted by the publisher or author.

Publishing Service By: Pen Legacy®
Cover & Formatting By: Junnita Jackson
Edited By: Carla Rigdon

Library of Congress Cataloging – in- Publication Data has been applied for.

Paperback ISBN: 978-1-7358798-8-8

PRINTED IN THE UNITED STATES OF AMERICA.

Throughout the Bible, the name of God is declared thousands of times. Whether Jehovah, Adonai, Abba or Yahweh, His name is Alpha and Omega – the beginning and the end; and in between, there are numerous Biblical leaders who made a royal imprint so profound, their blessings paved the way for generations to come. I want to highlight these royal leaders and the biblical principles which helped them stand out and rise up.

I pray to divinely guide you to shift into overflow through the pages of this devotion. Thank you for taking this journey with me. Prayerfully, you will receive a revelation that will strengthen your faith and ignite your God-given purpose. I am grateful for the others who went before us in great sacrifice, so that we may glean from them today. Their wise decisions led to wealthy lifestyles; I am not sharing their stories in any particular order.

Take the time to study the stories of each mentor, who remained focused on their God-givens task as written in Ecclesiastes 3. Their leadership styles exemplify the power of one person, who was *necessary*. By the end of this devotion, you will be inspired to stay on your course and live out your purpose. We all have been called to do something amazing. Be open to allowing God to light your path of success and fulfillment. God's only request is that we focus on Him in order to achieve the purpose He has planned for us. As you read these devotions, my prayer is that you experience breakthrough and freedom. Ask and seek, wisdom, and believe for revelation and truth to guide you. Remember **you are necessary!** God has hand selected you to be the answer others will glean from for generations to come.

Dinah: The Chosen One

Chosen by God to be set apart and the highlight of her father Jacob's life, Dinah's story comes roaring from the pages of Genesis 30:21. As Jacob's only daughter by Leah, Dinah's brothers honored and protected her; favor preceded her steps, and she was greatly loved all of her years.

Imagine being declared royalty before being born, because God called you blessed from the womb. Being adored and well cared for, because it's your pre-determined destiny. This is God's desire for us – to feel loved and cherished all of our days. From this day forward, think of yourself as a royal rebel like Dinah. You were born to be set apart; envision your life purpose as such. Chosen One, you are a reflection of God's marvelous light. When you open your eyes in the morning, know that you are blessed. Today, receive your calling and purpose as an honor you get to live out.

Declare with me: *I have been selected to be different from the rest.*

What did you glean from Dinah's Story?

_____
_____
_____
_____
_____
_____
_____
_____
_____

How do you see yourself as selected and chosen?

_____
_____
_____
_____
_____
_____
_____
_____
_____
_____

Caleb: Boldness is Necessary
"We are well capable of taking the land." **Numbers 13:30**

Along with Joshua, Caleb was only one of two men in the book of Numbers who entered the Promised Land. There's so much to learn from Caleb and his righteous boldness. First, he was bold enough to *believe*. Caleb's boldness may not have convinced the people, but God honored his radical belief. As a result, he and Joshua received the land as they envisioned.

What is your vision that others might not believe?

We no longer need permission from anyone to believe in our dreams for them to come to pass, no matter the size. Furthermore, validation from man is not required to enjoy the promises God has in store for us. Caleb said, "Let us go up at once and take possession for we are well able to overcome it." He was right! Let's keep that same perspective too. We are more than capable of possessing the land that God has given us. Seek God and He will direct your path. Now is the time to live prosperously and successfully…*God's way*. Expect a harvest!

Declare with me: *I will be bold enough to believe for all the promises God has for me!*

How did Caleb inspire you to speak boldly even when others didn't believe?

_____
_____
_____
_____
_____
_____
_____
_____
_____

What are you believing God for now?

_____
_____
_____
_____
_____
_____
_____
_____
_____
_____

Ezekiel 16:9 - I Am Anointed

You are anointed! God washed and anointed you with His oil.

Ezekiel was a prophet who spoke only what God commanded him to say. As a prophet, there were numerous times when Ezekiel witnessed God heal and breathe life into His children. He was anointed to build people up for the Kingdom of God, and so are we. As such, we should make our life's goal to be our best, anointed selves, and let the oil freely flow.

Please believe, God trusts us! He can use you to save and heal others. Ezekiel's purpose was to go where God sent him and tell the people what God said. We should glean from him and do the same. Go where God says go, and do what God says to do; expect results like Ezekiel experienced. Dry bones will live, and a great army will rise up for the Kingdom. Today, align your life with your anointing, and don't veer from it. The anointing only flows when activated. Activate the power within you and watch the oil continue flowing out of you.

Declare with me: *I am anointed to bless others.*

What are you anointed to do in this season of your life?

_____
_____
_____
_____
_____
_____
_____
_____
_____

How can you be a blessing to someone today?

_____
_____
_____
_____
_____
_____
_____
_____
_____

Isaac Blessed and Prosperous
"Be Blessed of the Lord." *Genesis 26:29*

Isaac was an extremely wealthy man whose anointing others attempted to stop, using various methods of cluttering his wells to block him from prospering. However, the favor Isaac had with God kept him prosperous in spite of their efforts. See, God wants us to be prosperous and kept by Him, not broke and bound. The majority of my life I was broke, because I believed others cluttered my well. I believed this was my fate to live in poverty, because my enemies stole the wealth that was intended for me. Listen, God's favor was so heavy on Isaac, others had to find him to make peace. Through Isaac's story, I learned to keep digging until you discover *Rehoboth* (a large place) and allow God's favor to fall fresh on you, even when it feels like the well has run dry.

It may take some time for others to realize God is with you, but don't allow man's view to stop you from growing. Keep God's power flowing through you, because it will lead you to harvest the wealth, He has for you. The way we maintain the anointing is by seeking creative and innovative ways to live. Declare today you are blessed of the Lord.

Declare with me: *I am blessed and prosperous.*

In what ways do others seek for you to be an answer for them?

_____
_____
_____
_____
_____
_____
_____
_____
_____

Do you believe that you are blessed and prosperous? Why, or why not?

_____
_____
_____
_____
_____
_____
_____
_____
_____
_____

Amos - Visionary of the Future

"Behold, the days are coming when blessing shall overtake the reaper." *Amos 9:13*

Amos was another prophet who was obedient to the voice of God. He was a visionary and speaker, communicating future events to all who would take heed. His focus was for children of God to be reapers. You are created to be a reaper, divinely called to live in the overflow. God intends for us to be so blessed; to share our overflow. We have all-access to what I like to call the *plenty-flow*, also known as the Bible. There are over 8,000 promises in the Bible, detailing plenty of promises for you to manifest.

Believe you will reap the harvest of all you have sown, and all God has promised. Amos spoke and believed for you to prosper. He visualized your harvest, so make room for it. Expect to be overtaken with blessings, as Amos declared. The prophet Amos said it, now all you have to do is receive it!

Declare with me: *I receive the blessing and all God has in store for me.*

What vision do you see for your family?

_____
_____
_____
_____
_____
_____
_____
_____
_____

Name a way you expect a harvest.

_____
_____
_____
_____
_____
_____
_____
_____
_____
_____
_____

Paul: By Faith

"Faith is going to lead you there... the just shall live by faith." ***Romans 1:17***

Paul was an influencer and instructor who created a roadmap for believers to follow. Think of it as a compass for us, who walk by faith. Paul provided us with instructions, dictating how to live by faith in spite of our circumstances. Paul was so filled with faith, half his writings were written from a jail cell. Some may think prison is the worst place to write about joy and faith. Paul kept his mind on doing the Father's will in spite of his location and his grim circumstances.

He spoke with confidence, fire, and zeal which extends to readers of his work. Whatever you are facing, face it from the eyes of freedom. Look to Paul's wisdom for faith to believe when times get hard. Children of God are called to live by faith; all we have to do is believe. Believe God is with you, no matter your situation. He will get the total glory from everything you face. By faith you will win, it shall come to pass, and victory is yours.

Declare with me: *I will live by faith, knowing God is with me.*

Name something that has not happened yet that you see happening for you?

_____
_____
_____
_____
_____
_____
_____
_____
_____

How can you - by faith, put in the work needed to reach that goal?

_____
_____
_____
_____
_____
_____
_____
_____
_____

Jeremiah: Next Level Performance

Then the Lord said to me, " You have seen well for I am ready to perform My Word." *Jeremiah 1:12*

Jeremiah heard from God at a young age, then proceeded to obey the voice of the Lord all the days of his life. God still seeks obedient leaders who desire to see, hear, and do only that which He speaks. Will you be one of the chosen God can use to perform His Word through? This assignment means you get to be God's spokesperson and ambassador for the Kingdom, and those things you speak out of obedience shall manifest. You will be Christ's very own representative.

God can perform miracles without our help; however, He has chosen to include us in His performance. Like Jeremiah, all the things you say shall come to pass. Your journey is filled with promises that you've spoken, and will be revealed God's way, in His perfect timing. Focusing on what you hear from Him makes us more mindful of what we say.

"The power of life and death are in your tongue." (*Deuteronomy 30:19*) Speak life! You have been recruited to be a witness for the Kingdom of God. Thank you, Jeremiah, for going before us to see how God will perform what you have seen.

Declare with me: *God, please trust me to speak that which You shall perform.*

What do you see in the Spirit that you can do?

_____
_____
_____
_____
_____
_____
_____
_____
_____

Ask God what He wants to do through you and write it here.

_____
_____
_____
_____
_____
_____
_____
_____
_____
_____

Joseph: New Foundation of Wealth

"…and I will provide for you and your little ones."
Genesis 50:21

In the Bible, Joseph experienced many "failures." He was thrown in a well, seduced by a treacherous woman in the home where he lived, went to prison - need I say more? But despite his trials, Joseph was a leader who saw "failing" as a means to success.

Every time Joseph found himself in the pit, he didn't remain there long. See, failure equipped Joseph to rise above the grim circumstances he faced, transforming his challenges into opportunities. He remained focused on the outcome, not the situation being used to sharpen him. From Joseph, we learn that endurance is one of the key factors to success. Joseph wound up running a nation he wasn't born into and did so successfully. Eventually, that success led him back to his family. In the end, Joseph provided for all of his siblings and their children.

Be willing to be the foundation for your family's empire. Wealth will be created from the paths you light, and through you, all the families of the earth shall be blessed. *(Genesis 12:3)*. Expect to be the chosen one sent to a birth a new funnel of wealth for your family and enjoy God's favor!

Declare with me: *I am the new founder of wealth in my family.*

Do you believe that you have been chosen by God?

_____
_____
_____
_____
_____
_____
_____
_____
_____

Are you okay with being the Chosen One?

_____
_____
_____
_____
_____
_____
_____
_____
_____
_____

Moses: God's Way of Wealth

"The Lord said, but I will harden his heart." *Exodus 4: 21*

As I studied Moses's story, I saw how God kept warning Moses that He was going to harden Pharaoh's heart. Moses had to repeatedly ask Pharaoh to let the people go, knowing Pharaoh would continuously deny his pleas. Imagine being sent to make the same request over and over, only to be denied. If you stop at this point in the story, you'll be confused, wondering why Moses had to go through the process. However, God sent Moses because His plan was to destroy the very idol sent to destroy God's children and His kingdom.

Despite the pain he endured, Moses remained faithful to God's instructions. Today, God is asking us to remain focused on the generational outcome, not simply the vision you are walking out now. We are Kingdom builders, just like Moses. Envision yourself as he did: a humble servant, bold leader, and warrior for the promises of God. When God finished with Pharaoh, He stripped his wealth and drowned his leaders in the Red Sea. God has a plan for us. Stick to it until the end, because the reward you will receive is priceless.

Declare with me: *I shall stay focused on God's abundance for me and future generations that will be revealed.*

Can you name something you desire that looks like it's not happening for you?

_____
_____
_____
_____
_____
_____
_____
_____
_____

Does Moses's perspective transform your way of thinking?

_____
_____
_____
_____
_____
_____
_____
_____
_____
_____

Eve: You are Necessary
"She shall be called woman." ***Genesis 2:23***

    Eve was born from man's need to be fulfilled. Guess what? We are too. Our lives were purposed before our arrival, so be your amazing self! Eve was God's response to Adam's void.

    Think about your business, family, career, and all the facets of your life. You are *necessary*. One thing we can gain from Eve's story is noting her lack of competition. She was designed to answer *The Call* no one else could. From this day forward, embrace Eve's destiny for yourself. You have no competition when you do you. Nobody else can do it like you do it. Eve paved the way for us to live life unapologetically as God's sent ones. Be all you are sent to become. You are the answer.

Declare with me: *I am necessary.*

Do you believe you are someone's missing link?

_____
_____
_____
_____
_____
_____
_____
_____
_____
_____

Can you strive to be the answer for someone today?

_____
_____
_____
_____
_____
_____
_____
_____
_____
_____

Live as You are Called
"The Lord has called each one, so let him walk." *1 Corinthians 7:17*

This scripture reminds us that we all have a call to fulfill. I genuinely enjoyed the TPT translation of the same scripture: *"May all believers continue to live the wonderful lives God has called them to live according to what He assigns."* You were created to be fulfilled, living life led by purpose. You are a divine answer.

This devotion was written to strengthen, teach, and align us with the Word of God. Thank you for this opportunity to serve you and enrich your spiritual perspective. Let's grow together and apply the biblical principles God has revealed to us. Prayerfully, something stands out to remind you that you are necessary, and because of you, others will be blessed. Jesus is ready and available to guide you all the way to a prosperous lifestyle. *Kingdom style.* I love you, moreover; God loves you, too. Remember you are loved.

Declare with me: *I am called and fulfilled to live a prosperous life.*

Do you believe that you are called?

_____
_____
_____
_____
_____
_____
_____
_____
_____

Take a moment to reflect on your calling.

_____
_____
_____
_____
_____
_____
_____
_____
_____

Abram: Made to Multiply

"I will make you a great nation and bless you." ***Genesis 12:2***

What if I told you that you were born to be great and do great things? Would you believe me? Well, it's true. Abram was a father to nations; since we are a part of the Kingdom of God, greatness is in your DNA. Don't settle or see yourself as anything but great. Abram's blessings are flowing through you, and God's blessings are in you too.

Expect a double portion of blessings and get ready for overflow. Greater things are headed your way - all you have to do is receive. Seek the *best*. In his latter years, Abram was so blessed, his favor still flows through us till this day. Abram multiplied; remember you are part of the blessed nation that keeps flowing and multiplying.

Declare with me: *I will be great all the days of my life!*

Do you agree that nations are blessed through you?

_____
_____
_____
_____
_____
_____
_____
_____
_____

How will you keep God's blessings flowing like Abram?

_____
_____
_____
_____
_____
_____
_____
_____
_____

Time to Return
"Each of you return to your family." ***Leviticus 25:10***

    I like to believe that in 2020, the world has been reset. COVID-19 was sent to revive the significance of family again. For months, the world was confined to their homes, only to be in the company of immediate family. With businesses closed, and even the churches shut down, we've been forced to stay inside with our loved ones. This is our opportunity to love each other again.

    In Leviticus 25:10 - the year of Jubilee, everyone returned to their families. Could this be what God is training us to do now? Could it be God is encouraging us to rebuild broken relationships? To reconnect in ways, we were too busy to do before? The *great return* is what I call this season we're in. Return to putting family first (after God). Establish family bonds. Bonds created to redesign and redefine what family will mean from here, for generations to come. This is the time to view your family as the golden ticket paving the way for others to succeed. Returning to your family brings healing to this nation. Keep family a priority!

Declare with me: *I will redefine the success of my family's future.*

In what way has Covid-19 led you to putting family first?

_____
_____
_____
_____
_____
_____
_____
_____

How is your family a priority for you from this day forward?

_____
_____
_____
_____
_____
_____
_____
_____

Saving the Next Generation

"Blessed is your advice and blessed are you." *1 Samuel 25:33*

Abigail is a true hero. Her quick action and divine wisdom saved her family from death. Her husband – Nabal, ignored David's request for food. The abrupt denial enraged David, who prepared his army to wipe out Nabal and Abigail's entire generation. Abigail received word of her husband's offense, and sprang into action, meeting David and assuming responsibility for Nabal's near fatal blunder, prompting David to spare their lives.

Please understand as the Body of Christ, God has blessed us with the wisdom to help rescue His children. David told Abigail, "Because of you, I made the right choice." The power of our words can shift chaos into order. Because of you, people can see the glory of the Lord being revealed. Speak! Abigail's heroic effort strengthened me to act fearlessly, too. Don't hope a leader will get it right; God could be positioning you to orchestrate the right outcome on behalf of everyone.

Declare with me: God, put the words in my mouth that will save others.

Can you see how God has blessed you to be a blessing to generations?

_____
_____
_____
_____
_____
_____
_____
_____
_____
_____

Name one way you feel you are a blessing.

_____
_____
_____
_____
_____
_____
_____
_____
_____
_____

Proverbs 3:3 - Mercy and Truth

"Let not mercy and truth forsake you, write them on the tablet your heart."

Mercy is defined as compassion shown towards someone whom it is within their power to punish or harm. Proverbs 3:3 encourages us to allow compassion and truth of the Word of God to rest on our hearts, so we won't forget we have two options to choose from: chaos or order. Mercy dictates knowing someone hurt us, but we must forgive them anyway; truth is necessary when we could seek revenge but choose not to.

Our relationship with God should direct our responses to circumstances. One of the reasons God says, "bind them on your neck," is because we have to forgive a lifetime of hurt. Compassion is required daily, to help us keep moving forward; show compassion for others consistently. When coupled together, mercy and truth leads you to favor and high esteem with God and men. Let truth and mercy free you indeed!

Declare with me: *I forgive because I know the truth.*

What does mercy mean to you?

_____
_____
_____
_____
_____
_____
_____
_____

What does truth mean to you?

_____
_____
_____
_____
_____
_____
_____
_____
_____

No More Childish Ways

"When I was child, I acted like a child, but now I have put away childish ways."
1 Corinthians 13:11

It's time to abandon immature thoughts we grew up believing were right. As the Bible says in 1 Corinthians 13:11, "When I was a child, I spoke and thought as a child. When I became a man/woman, I put away childish things." What childish thoughts have you outgrown? Mine was impoverished thinking. All my life, my family made poverty a lifestyle, and it stuck with me. I grew up believing struggling was a means of survival, but I've finally come to the conclusion it's time to put away that toxic childish mentality.

The shift happened when I started believing the Word of God over generational curses. I'm persuaded that from this day forward, I will no longer be bound to struggle. No more just getting by, nor living check to check, or scouring for discounts. I had to press delete on this mindset. Reading scriptures about wealth upgrades your mindset. Reading and believing what God says about my wealth deletes the past. He said, "I will give you the power to get the wealth." (***Det. 8:18***). I challenge you to upgrade your juvenile thoughts with His Word. It's time to upgrade our minds to the new level God is elevating us to. What thoughts are you willing to let go of today in order to embrace all God has for you now? His overflow awaits those who are ready to receive it; all He requires of you is to put away childish things.

Declare with me: *I am available for God's abundance.*

Name some childish thinking you will release today?

_____
_____
_____
_____
_____
_____
_____
_____
_____
_____

What comes to mind when you think abundance?

_____
_____
_____
_____
_____
_____
_____
_____
_____
_____

Jesus: Future Focus
"And Jesus grew." *Luke 2:52*

Jesus was born to show us how to live. He gave us the path to growth and favor and provided His expertise on living holy. I love reading about Jesus because He focused on the future. He lived for our future, for you and me to live abundantly and free. I urge you to view your life as a gift. We get to live because Jesus gifted His life to shield us from sin. Every day of His life was lived with you in mind. He took the pain so you and I can be pain free. Jesus covered the cost so we can release the past. Let it go.

Jesus wants complete access to you. That access granted means accepting Him as your savior; He'll do the rest. I love how no matter where you find yourself in life, Jesus effortlessly carries your burdens. Surrender it all to him, because my friend, believing in Him means an amazing future for you. Through Christ, you can do all things (*Philippians 4:13*). What a relief knowing that we no longer have to worry, live in fear, or doubt. Jesus can handle it all for you.

Declare with me: *I have a great future ahead of me, thanks to Jesus.*

Name a future accomplishment you desire to achieve?

Will you trust Jesus to get you there?

Elisha - Made Alive

"The dead man touched Elisha...the man was revived and stood." 2 Kings 13:21

Elisha was a powerful prophet, and mighty warrior for the Kingdom of God. Often when he spoke, Elisha's prophecies didn't make sense to others, but they worked. He was so mighty; kings sought his anointing and power. Even after his death, the anointing remained so heavy on Elisha, that a dead man was laid on his bones. Suddenly, the dead man was revived and stood to his feet.

Elisha was a Man of God who was faithfully Spirit-filled and God led. We can glean from his character, performing the will of God, too. I declare and decree God has a great work for us to do. Throughout Elisha's life, people were strengthened, led in the truth, and healed. We have access to that same power and anointing through Jesus. Activate your power! God will back up every word He gives you to share.

Declare with me: *I have the power within me to revive others.*

Name something you know God delivered you from.

_____
_____
_____
_____
_____
_____
_____
_____
_____
_____
_____

Name something you seek to rise above now.

_____
_____
_____
_____
_____
_____
_____
_____
_____
_____

Rahab: The One Who Believed

"By faith Rahab did not perish...she was received with peace." *Hebrews 11:31*

Rahab was a genius. Upon hearing spies were invading the town where she lived, Rahab made the decision to believe God over what others believed in her city, and used her faith to rescue her family with God's protection as Joshua and his army destroyed the entire city next to them. All it takes is to believe, and one can save their family. We have a choice - will we believe God or will we die in defeat? Your faith can lay the foundation for future generations to follow, as Rahab did for her son Boaz. Boaz loved God and was wealthy. His prosperity was made possible because of her belief. Be the one to save your next generation through believing God and His righteousness, and everything else will be added. (*Matthew 6:33*)

Declare with me: *I will believe God.*

What is something you are believing in for your family?

_____
_____
_____
_____
_____
_____
_____
_____
_____
_____

Will you keep the faith until what you are believing happens?

_____
_____
_____
_____
_____
_____
_____
_____
_____
_____

Daniel

"So, this Daniel prospered in the reign of Darius." ***Daniel 7:28***

Daniel was the leader of all leaders. He outlived the reign of three kings and remained the same through each one of them. Many people tried to destroy Daniel; his faith and confidence in God kept him alive through every plot others pitted against Him. The last king - Darius, loved Daniel. Because of his favor with the king, other men envied Daniel and created a law that he could not pray to God. Instead of bowing to their demands, Daniel chose to remain obedient to God and was thrown in the lion's den to die. But God put a shield of protection all around Daniel, and he survived.

Daniel's unwavering faith changed the belief of the one king, who made a decree that all the people respect and honor the God of Daniel. Royal Rebels, as you can see through this devotion, it only takes one to believe for nations to be saved. Be the person who believes God will take care of you, no matter what. Daniel stayed focused on the truth. May I recommend we do the same? Trust and believe. Through us, others will come to know Christ and see the glory of the Lord.

Declare with me: *I will prosper, because I believe God.*

Name something you believe that others do not.

Can you name another way?

Kingdom and Power
"For yours is the kingdom, power, and the glory forever."
Matthew 6:13

In the Kingdom, we have all access to do miraculous works with power. We're able to level up to our divine connection and a powerful lifestyle for the Kingdom. All we have to do is seek God's path for our lives and stay on it. God has equipped us with the tools to be amazing! He plants us to live right and bloom. Throughout the Bible, there's story after story of chosen children with the same goal of leading others to the promises of God.

We aren't born with basic knowledge; we enter this world powerless. However, we don't have to remain powerless, unsure, and misdirected. Today, declare and decree that you will activate and access the power God instills in you. Ask God first, then obey His instructions and use your power effectively. His power and glory within you will last forever. *Thank You for the power to do great things, Lord.*

Enjoy being the new normal! Jesus has given you permission to live powerfully for the Kingdom. Arise!

Declare with me: *I am filled with His glorious power.*

Do you believe you are powerful? How?

___

Do you stand strong in that authority? Briefly describe how.

___

Joshua: The Complete Crossover
"All crossed over on dry ground, completely." *Joshua 3:17*

Joshua helped the Children of Israel over dry land to the Jordan River. Along with Caleb, he entered into The Promised Land. Consider for a moment, out of millions of people – there were only two who entered to the next level of prosperity. May I inspire you through Joshua's story? It's time to cross over! Cross over into what, you might ask?

Cross over into a greater way of thinking, and cross over into generational blessings for your family. Cross over to your royal status. Cross over to love and favor. Furthermore, cross over to speaking truth to yourself and those around you. God parted the river for His children to completely cross over so that we may live in abundance. We have to know that those who went before us paved the way so we may be fulfilled. Today, receive the crossover. Ask God to help you cross over to the next level of you.

Declare with me: *I will cross over to the Kingdom, completely.*

What are you willing to let go of to embrace your Kingdom lifestyle?

_____
_____
_____
_____
_____
_____
_____
_____
_____

Will you cross over to your next level of success?

_____
_____
_____
_____
_____
_____
_____
_____
_____
_____

10 and 1

"And one of them, when saw he was healed, gave thanks."
Luke 17:15

Ten lepers had an encounter with Jesus, who healed all of them at once, then instructed them to go and tell the priest. Unfortunately, only one of the men came back and gave thanks. That man was healed and made whole, because of his gratitude. Being thankful goes along way. Jesus said to the man, "Arise, go your way. Your faith has made you well."

By faith give thanks, knowing Jesus has healed you. I love how the man returned alone, knowing it was the wise thing to do. Let wisdom be your guide, even if you are the only wise one. Be the one who does what is right. Be the one who may have to walk alone. Give thanks in everything. You are the one! God is always healing, and He gives wholeness to those with a thankful heart.

Declare with me: *Be grateful and give thanks.*

What are you thankful for?

_____
_____
_____
_____
_____
_____
_____
_____
_____
_____

How has God blessed you lately?

_____
_____
_____
_____
_____
_____
_____
_____
_____
_____

Nehemiah 1:10 – I've Been Redeemed

"Now these are your people, redeemed by your great power."

Nehemiah remained focused to get things done right. He viewed his God-given task as the only mission he was sent to complete, and fervently prayed and fasted for others. What can we learn from Nehemiah? He was created to be the answer to someone's prayer. In 52 days, Nehemiah prayed, built a team, and unified a community. Together, they built a wall of protection to protect generations to come.

Nehemiah didn't even live there; however, God placed the mission on his heart and he fulfilled it. What have you been sent to fulfill? Are you focused on completing that mission? If not, start now and remain focused until you know your mission is complete.

God has given me a mission to awaken and equip families to build bonds worthy of continuing. It might take me a lifetime to do it, but with God, I know it shall be done. I am believing in *sudden* results. If you are uncertain about your journey, pray and ask God what your mission is, then remain focused and complete it! Whatever it is, God shall supply all you need to finish.

Declare with me: *I am a child of God, sent to redeem.*

Are you willing to go where God sends you?

Are you willing to serve God's people, no matter who it is?

Prosper & Multiply

"You shall possess it... He will prosper you and multiply you." ***Deuteronomy 30: 5***

It's time to prosper and multiply! To prosper means succeed and grow; to multiply means increasing in numbers. Marrying the two together according to the Word of God, you can expect to succeed and see increase. Keep in mind, thinking big about prospering and multiplying is more than just money...it's a lifestyle. The more you prosper and multiply, ask God to give you the wisdom to produce double no matter what your dreams or goals are. I've learned that dreaming too small was hindering me. My tiny goals didn't outweigh God's destiny for me.

May I challenge you not to set small goals for yourself the way I did? See, for years, my biggest goal was to pay my bills on time. That was it. Now, I've expanded my dreamy mindset to include paying off the debts of others such as their houses, school tuition, and more. We were created for more and should act on it now. *Multiply* your thinking. Expect your family to live in the overflow. He's done it for others – believe God can prosper and multiply you, too!

Declare with me: *I believe I will prosper and multiply!*

Name a way you want to experience increase?

_____
_____
_____
_____
_____
_____
_____
_____
_____
_____

Do you believe you will prosper according to your belief?

_____
_____
_____
_____
_____
_____
_____
_____
_____
_____

Peace and Prosperity

"Seek the peace and prosperity from that city." *Jeremiah 29:7*

In this verse, we are challenged to seek peace and prosperity through a city, expecting abundance if that is where God sent you. Throughout the Bible, God sent His children to countries where He blessed them, most of which were places they didn't know. My prayer for future generations is that we go where we are sent obediently. Like those children in the Bible who expected to reap a harvest in their new city, we can expect the same in ours. Peace settles where God sends us; let's pray:

God I thank You for divine growth and prosperity. Please reveal where I am supposed to be. From this day forward, be at peace knowing there is overflow available where you are sent.

Declare with me: *I seek prayer, peace, and prosperity.*

What does God's peace mean to you?

___

Through the reading of this devotional, can you see how God wants you to prosper?

___

Jeremiah 8:23-Arise & Go

"Arise and go down to the potter's house, and there you will hear my word."

    If God told you to *arise and go*, would you? God commands to *arise and go* 147 times in the Bible; He wants us to keep growing and moving forward. He strongly suggested to the children of the Bible to *arise and go* where He sent them, and they did just that.

    Today, can we as believers do the same immediately upon hearing His command? The command given by God in Jeremiah caused the children to hear His Word. Today, God has made it easier for us to hear Him through our personal relationship with Him. During our quiet time, He downloads revelation for us to follow. Arise now, seek Him in prayer, and you will hear His word.

Declare with me: *I will arise and go where God sends me.*

In what way is God calling you now?

What revelation have you received lately?

You are God's New Thing

"Don't remember the former things, behold I am doing a new thing. Now it shall spring forth." *Isaiah 43:18-19*

    I have an announcement to make: You have been promoted! Today marks the day that you will put your past behind you. All you've gone through was to mold you into the person you are today. Press delete!
    Transform your new mindset to believe in abundance. God has more in store for you to experience than what you think; however, your mind needs to be open to receive it. Embrace yourself as God's new thing. He wants to use you for His favor and glory. You are a living testimony that the Word of God works.

Declare with me: I am God's new thing. I will be the new normal.

Abundance is awaiting your arrival - will you receive it?

Matthew 6:33

"Seek first the kingdom of God, His righteousness and everything else will be added."

We are blueprints of God's image. He orders your future steps, and the path you should follow. He only requests that you seek Him for direction. God desires you to experience overflow. Your cup should be running over with blessings to share with others. As you seek God's will for your life and obey His instruction, everything else will be added to you. *Everything.* God has a system in place for you to stay connected to Him.

Align your heart with His will; His plans for you will take your lifetime to complete. The best part? Your overflow will continue spilling over to generations after you.

Declare with me: I will seek God's will first, so everything else shall be added for me.

What do you want to add to your life?

_____
_____
_____
_____
_____
_____
_____
_____
_____
_____
_____
_____
_____

Genesis 12:11-13

"It may be well with me for your sake and that I may live because of you..."

Abram and his wife Sarai were entering into a foreign land. Knowing his wife was beautiful and other men would desire her, Abram asked Sarai to lie, so that they would not kill him to have her. At the end of verse 13, Abram said to his wife, "Because of you I may live." What power for one woman to have. Sarai was so striking, her husband feared for his life.

We have that same power and authority as Sarai. You are necessary! You are beautiful, inside and out. Others live because of your presence. Be confident that you are the answer. Now is the time to live your life as the woman others need to succeed.

Declare with me: I am the woman that keeps others alive and successful.

In what way do you add value to others?

It's Time for Overflow

"All these blessings shall come upon you and overtake you." ***Deuteronomy 28:2-3***

I hear the sound of abundance. Expect a harvest! This devotional was written to remind us that we should expect to be blessed. Obedience attracts abundance. God has so much in store for you; don't make the level you are currently on your final stop.

Our next level of success is here. Let's journey together towards all things in abundance. You are a visionary and woman of influence - others will be blessed because of you. It's possible to thrive and make room for others to succeed. Believe that you will enter overflow and increase now. I decree and declare God will bless us indeed. Make room for overflow.

Declare with me: Overflow is headed my way abundantly. I am ready!

How will you prepare to receive your next level of increase?

Proverbs 31: Design
"You excel them all." ***Proverbs 31:29***

Wow! Spending this time with you through the pages of this book have been amazing! I have been enriched and challenged to believe on a higher level in faith. Have you?

Hopefully, you have been ignited to bloom in your purpose. You are the woman God has chosen. You are the new standard of excellence. You outclass them all. God is raising you up as a woman of power and authority who will guide others to their destiny. You are God's chosen vessel. You have no competition. God created you, then broke the mold. There will not be another person again like you. You shall outshine them all because only you can get it done. My friend, you are set apart. No one else will ever do what you do. May I challenge you to give life all you got from this day forward, since you are equipped to excel?

Declare with me: Others have done great things but I excel them all.

Name a powerful way you have excelled?

_____
_____
_____
_____
_____
_____
_____
_____
_____
_____
_____
_____
_____

Blessed Families

"And in you all the families of the earth shall be blessed."
Genesis 12:3

You are the one. Hand selected to be blessed. In you, others will be blessed because you are required to show up and deliver the goods - the goodness of your heart. Others will be blessed by your presence. God is trusting you to do all things through Him who strengthens you. "Speak Lord, your servant is listening." [*Add your name here*]. The blessings of the Lord are upon you. Remember, God will continue to strengthen you to be someone's answered prayer. Lives will be changed because of your gifts and talents.

Serve others with gladness. Souls will be healed through your voice. Families all around the world need you. Because of you, families around the world shall be blessed.

Declare with me: I am a blessing to many families and generations to come.

How will you light up the path for the next generation?

Cleansed Heart

"I will sprinkle clean water on you and give you a new heart." Ezekiel 36:25-28

God makes it His business to cleanse our hearts. God is amazing at broadening our perspective and has sprinkled clean water on your new heart and fresh spirit. Before you know it, you will have the heart to forgive those who hurt you, as well as a heart to forgive yourself for the hurt you might have done. Expect God to cleanse you of old mistakes, behavior and pain. Expect breakthrough and freedom. As you receive fresh revelation, walk out the full you. Give yourself permission to love and share your heart with others more.

Use God's spirit within you as your guide. Allow yourself to relish in your new heart for God's people. God has cleansed us, and our job is to stay clean through the reading of the Word.

Declare with me: I receive my new heart.

Describe the joy you are feeling right now?

Dry Bones Living Again

"I prophesied as He commended and breath came into them. They became a great army." *Ezekiel 37:10-14*

God gave Ezekiel power to breathe life into dry bones. Those bones grew into a great Army out of one man's obedience to breathe. God wants to use our breath, too. I am believing God to give us fresh anointing. You are powerful! Your words matter. Speak life into others through the knowledge of His word, and watch your great army grow. God has equipped the body of Christ to strengthen others to come back to life again.

I am so thankful for the person who took the time to speak life into me. Now, I get to be a part of the army of the Lord. God trusts that He can use us to be obedient voices who bring others back to life. God's spirit is alive in you! Moreover, give others the gift to live. *Just breathe.*

Declare with me: I will speak life into others.

In what way will you speak life into others?

Kingdom Restored

"I will restore my great army which I sent among you."
Joel 2:25-27

Here are ways of defining a great army for the Kingdom:
- Being Sent
- Satisfied
- Praise the name of the Lord your God
- Dealt with wondrously
- Never will be put to shame
- Knows that God is in their midst
- Knows there is no other God

Your great army is aware they are God's people – The spirit of God directs their path!

Declare with me: I am apart of God's Kingdom

What is your definition of the Kingdom?

The Cup Runs Over

"It is time to give out of your overflow of life, no longer out of the cup given to you for survival." **Psalms 23:5**

Reading the Word of God fills you daily. In Psalms 23, the author - David, shares how God's power overtook him with love. God's strength filled him up so much, David had to share it with others.

Let this inspire you to grow in the love of God to the point that the love you feel is experienced by others through you, too. You have so much to offer this world. No longer will you give out of your cup, but you will know where to obtain the supply to overflowing love - *Jesus Christ*. Let God fill you – your cup will run over.

Declare with me: I will give out my cup that overflows.

How will you keep your spirit filled?

Speak!

"Speak Lord, your servant is listening." *1 Samuel 3:7-11*

God continuously called Samuel, and the young boy went to Eli, unaware it wasn't Eli who called him. After the third time, Eli recognized Samuel was hearing the Voice of God and instructed the boy to listen. I love how consistent God is with us. He desires for us to hear our calling and answer accordingly.

God needs your voice, which has amazing power. Your power (voice) is required in this season, as others need the truth revealed to them. You are a divine service provider. Speak! Hearing and speaking what God says to you is your only requirement. God has already put the words in your mouth and will lead you to the person who shall receive it. Speak!

Lord give us this day our daily bread. Listen daily for what God has for you to do. Diligently seek to speak. It's your voice we need to hear.

Declare with me: Speak, Lord…your servant is listening.

What do you hear God saying to you lately?

God's Great Army

"They lived and stood upon their feet a great army"
Ezekiel 37:10

"We are God's great army who He has sent among the people to be satisfied, to be fulfilled, to be purpose led, to be the sent one, to win the war for the kingdom." *Ezekiel 37.*

The great thing about God's will is that He doesn't require you to fight or carry a weapon. The only equipment you need is prayer and surrendered heart. Prayer helps you aim right at your target; a surrendered heart keeps you obedient.

God, I thank You and trust You for Your divine will being done.
I surrender and trust in Your will.
In Jesus', name Amen.

Declare with me: I am a soldier in the army of the Lord.

What do you surrender in prayer?

Expect to be Restored
"So I will restore to you the years." ***Joel 2:25***

Expect Overflow! God is restoring our time, so let go of old things now – they have nothing to do with your new. Your past is gone. Overflow is asking permission to overtake you. Grant it access!

So, I will restore to you the years that the swarming locust has eaten, the crawling locust, consuming locust, and chewing locust.

I know many have experienced difficult childhoods, wondering how you can be restored. I have the answer. God is in the redeeming business, so let Him handle the how. The past is only a distraction because guess what - you are still here! Surrender and let go; God has a double portion waiting for you. As it says in *Joel 2:* "You shall eat in plenty and be satisfied. Praise the name of the Lord your God who has dealt wondrously with you. God's people shall never be put to shame."

Declare with me: I have been redeemed.

Increase!

"And Jesus increased in wisdom, stature, and in favor with God and men." **Luke 2:52**

You have grown in wisdom. Your status has been upgraded. Most of all, you have favor with God and men. Put it all together, and you share a similar same experience as Jesus: you are high class! Use this season wisely. Seek wisdom daily. Continuously make room for expansion. Keep a grateful heart and watch how favor follows you.

Expect the power to obtain wealth, and divine direction to properly steward over it. Increase comes with purpose. Always set goals and keep them before you. Your goals will create financial flow.

Declare with me: I will increase in wisdom, status, and favor.

Jot down how you have experienced growth?

Do Not Worry

"And do not seek what you should eat or drink, nor have an anxious mind." *Luke 12:29*

Did you know that "do not worry" can be found in the Bible 365 times? This should remind you with each passing day, you don't have to be anxious. Worry is a distraction from the truth being revealed. Every day, seek first the Kingdom and God's will for your life. Everything else you need will be added. (*Matthew 6:33*). Know that the solution you need will be revealed in due time. Yes, you will still have concerns. Yes, uncertainty will sometimes remain...don't let that stop you.

Develop the mind of Christ and cast your cares on Him. He will lead you to your solution. From this moment on, remember - do not worry. Instead, seek God's will. Let Him be the GPS in every situation.

Declare with me: I will not worry because God can handle it.

What will have been consumed by? Release it!

Faith

"Now faith is the substance of things hoped for and the evidence of things not seen." ***Hebrews 11:1***

We are ambassadors of faith, Kingdom representatives that God's Word works! Your faith is an honorable badge that you have earned. Your faith is so strong, it can provoke others to believe, too.

God has partnered with you through your faith. When you hope for something according to God's will, He will allow it to manifest. Keep your faith in motion, by believing in something BIG…*no limits*. You don't have to know all the details, just have the faith to believe God will reveal and supply. Your faith is a powerful force that makes visions manifest.

Declare with me: I believe by faith it shall be done.

What are you believing for next by faith?

New Thing

"Behold I make all things new." *Revelation 21:5*

I love how God creates a new thing inside of people, starting with our hearts, cleansing and making them pure again. You might look and walk the same; however, you are no longer the same. When God changes your thoughts, He alters your response.

I can remember when that change happened to me. After surrendering my life to God, my newfound righteousness overtook the person I was. I found myself forgiving others, and I sought solutions instead of worrying about my problems. When God makes things new, you will no longer want to be who you were before. Receive your clean heart and welcome the new opportunities which come with it. New things are marvelous when God makes them possible.

Declare with me: I receive the renewing of my mind.

Write something new you will do for 2021?

Take the Lead

"So the Lord exalted Solomon exceedingly in the sight of all." *1 Chronicles 29:25*

It's time for you to take the lead. God is about to do some mighty things through you that no one else has seen, nor will they be able to say it has been done before.

Solomon was the only king whom God made exceedingly wise and blessed. In fact, Solomon was described as the wisest king ever known. Pray to God to make you exceedingly wise too. We need you! Arise and lead this nation to the promises of God. He will teach and give you wisdom beyond your years; you have been granted access on gaining wisdom when reading your Bible. Be the leader others can follow and glean from. You shall be prosperous and successful. From this day forward, believe you were born to take the lead.

Declare with me: I am a leader.

What lights you up when you're the leader?

Name something you are proud that you led or will lead next?

_____
_____
_____
_____
_____
_____
_____
_____
_____
_____
_____
_____
_____

No More

"Behold, I am doing a new thing shall you not know it."
Isaiah 43:18-19

Failure is the new success! We just experienced a reset around the world. Many systems people relied on failed. COVID-19 may have failed many; however, for you and me, it was God's way of setting us up to shine. God wants you to expand your voice globally.

Now, classes, events, celebrations and services have gone virtual. You can travel anywhere in the world from your computer. I'd like to challenge you to think globally and make a splash! It is time for you to be seen. No more hiding your gifts. No more hiding behind the shadows of someone else's light. You are marvelous light. Shine baby, shine! Behold you are the new thing... now you know it.

Declare with me: **I am marvelous light.**

How do you feel made new?

The Book of Nehemiah

"So, the wall was finished on the 25th day of Elul, in 52 days." **Nehemiah 6:15**

The book of Nehemiah is a book of restoration, demonstrating God's great works in record time. When I read the book of Nehemiah, I saw how God can use a single prayer warrior. Nehemiah's vision was to build a lifetime protection for a community of one. In 52 days, Nehemiah and his tribe built a wall that protected their generation and beyond.

Let your goal for success be greater than simply you. When we connect our vision with God's power, we have the ability to do exceedingly above what we can imagine. *(Ephesian 3:20)* What idea do you have that can generate a lifetime support for others?

As you are called to strengthen many people, you have to plan accordingly. In return, watch God bless your faithfulness. When birthing a dream of this magnitude, expect results in record time.

Declare with me: **I will complete goals in record time.**

Write out a goal you have that you want completed.

Breakthrough

"Know the truth and the truth shall make you free.
" *John 8:32*

It's time to experience a breakthrough. For years, my family and I lived paycheck to paycheck, all the while, my taste for success kept growing, but I ignored the thirst.

Breakthrough happened for me when I stopped being fine with just getting by. One of the major reasons I stayed broke for so long, was because of my surroundings. I grew up watching my family and friends hustle to survive, so I assumed I was supposed to do the same. Suddenly…the awakening happened. I declared I would not be broke any longer. Breakthrough!

Will you join me in this declaration? Aligning yourself with like-minded people brings about breakthroughs. Being in the presence of successful people, watching them closing business deals, buying land, and etc. inspires you to grow. Most of all, set you free from self-imposed limitations. May I challenge you to invest in a program or group to expand your growth? God wants us to be blessed. Let's grow.

Declare with me: I am ready for breakthrough and freedom.

Jot down the areas where you need a breakthrough.

_____
_____
_____
_____
_____
_____
_____
_____
_____
_____
_____
_____
_____
_____
_____
_____

Be the First

"So the Lord exalted Solomon exceedingly in the sight of all." **1 Chronicles 29:25**

What God is about to do through you, others have not seen or done before. Stop trying to look for examples - **you are it!** You are creating a new mantle of success. The Lord exalted Solomon with royal power. You have that same royal power within. Now is the time to activate your power! Royal power comes from a personal relationship with God. Solomon consistently asked God for divine direction in all of his decisions. Consequently, Solomon experienced an abundance of firsts and overflow.

Like Solomon, be bold enough to ask God to let you be *first*. You have been chosen to be the first in what you do.

Declare with me: I am honored to be the first_____.

Write a way you are the first in your family to do God's will.

Royal Crown

Esther obtained grace and favor in his sight.
Esther 2:17

He gave her the crown and she became queen.
Esther obtained favor with all who saw her. For the rest of her life she wore a crown. Forever, she was queen.
What an honor to know we too have been crowned. God has handpicked you and me for royalty. We have obtained unlimited grace and favor.
Will you wear the crown?
Will you walk out your queenship?
You are chosen and loved.
This is a friendly reminder you have been crowned. Wear it with dignity and favor. Expect a harvest, overflow is headed your way… all because of your crown.
Others will see and know that you are royalty, will you receive it?

Declare with me: I will wear my royal crown a lifetime.

Do you have the faith that you have been crowned?

Clothed in Righteousness

"Strength and honor are her clothing, she shall rejoice in time to come." ***Proverbs 31:25***

I used to have a lot of clothes. I would wear them a couple times, then give them away - I've done this for years. Clothes can come and go. The clothing I'm talking about; however, today is *strength* and *honor*. Let strength and honor be your clothing, they are not for sale nor given away.

Strength keeps you going no matter what's going on around you. Honor comes with a standard of excellence you won't back down from. When the two combines, you are clothed with the right stuff. You can rejoice because you are covered through the blood of Jesus Christ.

Declare with me: I am clothed in strength and honor.

List 3 core values that strengthen you.

Global Imprint
"Go into all the World..." **Mark 16:15**

How will we know you were here on earth?

How did you use your gifts and talents globally?

May I challenge you to strive to create a global imprint?

You have been sent to impact nations, kingdoms, and empires. You might not know anyone globally, but your imprint can be known all around the world. Write books, teach courses, etc. In time, you will grow beyond those you know. No one else gets to experience being you. Be all you are destined to be. Everyone we read about in the Bible has made a global imprint, and so can you. God said go into all the world. There are over five billion people you can impact. Ask Him to make you global.

Declare with me: I will make a global impact.

What do you want to be known for globally?

Great Name

"Make your name great." ***Genesis 12:2***

In Genesis 12, God told Abram He would make Him a great nation and make his name great. Consequently, Abram became the father to nations.

Guess what?

You are a part of that nation.

You were created to have a great name.

From this day forward, be proud of your family. Create a family bond worthy of repeating.

God is going to bless you.

Arise and raise the bar of what your family's lineage will be known for.

Declare with me: I will build a great name for my family

What do you want to be known for when others speak about you?

Time to Accelerate

"Test all things, hold fast to what is good."
1 Thessalonians 5:21

You are ready to accelerate! As per the goal of this devotional, test the Word of God. The Bible is the best source to gain clarity and understanding. Keep reading it and learning the truth for yourself. Every answer you need can be found in His Word.

Before He formed you, God created a blueprint with all that you would need to succeed. Our job is to read the Bible, believe it, and accelerate to the next level of ourselves. I am so glad we have a place to go when we are unsure, need clarity, or are ready to receive God's blessings. The Bible has all of your answers; go forth and pass the test.

Declare with me: I will find my answers in the Word of God.

How do you want to grow?

You are Necessary

"Exceedingly grace of God in you." *2 Corinthians 9:14*

I am so glad that you were born. God made it His duty not to duplicate you. On the inside of you, there is a genius no one else can produce. What are you waiting for? You don't need permission from others; ask God what you are to become. Do not seek validation to be you. God is with you!

You are necessary everywhere and sent to do all your hands are set to do. You are necessary in your family. You are necessary in the community. Be someone else's necessary solution. God needs you! You are the one we will read about in the future, about how you blessed others, and the global imprint you made. Strive and thrive in all that will help you to be successful. Dream big enough that others will benefit from you for a lifetime.

Declare with me: I am Necessary and God's grace is flowing through me.

Name something you are proud of yourself for.

Wealth Generator

"You may be prosperous and successful." *Joshua 1:8*

This is the last day of our devotional. Can you believe it has been 60 days? It has been a delight to serve you, and my prayer is that you will set your heart and mind on all things abundance.

Remember: God wants us to be prosperous and successful. He has 8000 promises in the Bible for us to experience; it would take a lifetime to experience them all. Hopefully, this devotional will help you be mindful of the pieces going into abundant living:

Receive the power of a renewed mind.

Expect your heart to be cleansed by God.

Allow His spirit to be placed on the inside of you.

Give God permission to guide and direct your path, so that future generations will follow. You will be fruitful and continue to multiply the rest of your life. You are a wealth generator; expect a lifetime of harvest. Enjoy God's power and vision for you to be prosperous.

Declare with me: I am wealthy!

Thank you for taking the time to inject His word into your life today. I hope your confidence has been ignited and that you accelerate towards abundance as you pursue your purpose with excellence!

Let's keep in touch and continue to grow together:
Website: kendratc.com
Facebook: bit.ly/royalrc
Instagram: @kendrathorp

www.ingramcontent.com/pod-product-compliance
Lightning Source LLC
Chambersburg PA
CBHW030912080526
44589CB00010B/264